READY, SET, DRAW!
MONSTERS AND ROBOTS

AILIN CHAMBERS

W

FRANKLIN WATTS
LONDON • SYDNEY

First published in 2015 by Franklin Watts

Franklin Watts
338 Euston Road
London
NW1 3BH

Franklin Watts Australia
Level 17/207 Kent Street, Sydney, NSW 2000

Produced by Arcturus Publishing Limited,
26/27 Bickels Yard, 151–153 Bermondsey Street, London SE1 3HA

Editors: Samantha Hilton, Kate Overy and Joe Harris
Illustrations: Dynamo Limited
Design concept: Keith Williams
Design: Dynamo Limited and Notion Design
Cover design: Ian Winton

A CIP catalogue record for this book is available
from the British Library.

Dewey Decimal Classification Number 743.8
ISBN 978 1 4451 4189 3

Printed in China

SL003594UK

Supplier 03, Date 1214, Print run 3887

CONTENTS

GRAB THESE!

Are you ready to create some amazing pictures? Wait a minute! Before you begin drawing, you will need a few important pieces of equipment.

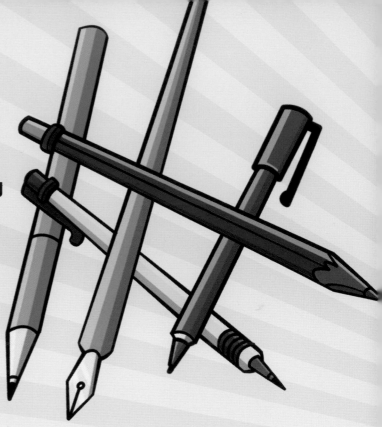

PENS AND PENCILS

You can use a variety of drawing tools including pens, chalks, pencils and paints. But to begin with use an ordinary HB pencil.

PAPER

Use a clean sheet of paper for your final drawings. Scrap paper is useful and cheap for your practice work.

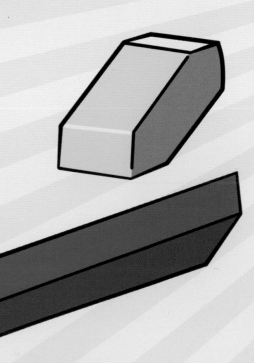

ERASERS

Everyone makes mistakes! That's why every artist has a good eraser. When you rub out a mistake, do it gently. Scrubbing hard at your paper will ruin your drawing and possibly even rip it.

RULER

Always use a ruler to draw straight lines.

COMPASS

You can use a compass to draw a perfect circle. However, some people find this tricky. Try drawing round a coin, bottle top or any other small, round item you can find.

INK PENS

The drawings in this book have been finished with an ink line to make them sharper and cleaner. You can get the same effect by using a ballpoint or felt-tip pen.

PAINT

Adding colour to your drawing brings it to life. You can use felt-tip pens, coloured pencils or water-based paints such as poster paints, which are easy to clean.

GETTING STARTED

In this book we use a simple two-colour system to show you how to draw a picture. Just remember: new lines are blue lines!

STARTING WITH STEP 1

The first lines you will draw are very simple shapes. They will be shown in blue, like this. You should draw them with a normal HB pencil.

ADDING MORE DETAIL

As you move on to the next step, the lines you have already drawn will be shown in black. The new lines for that stage will appear in blue.

FINISHING YOUR PICTURE

When you reach the final stage you will see the image in full colour with a black ink line. Inking a picture means tracing the main lines with a black pen. After the ink dries, use your eraser to remove all the pencil lines before adding your colour.

A texture is the way a surface looks and feels. It can be rough, smooth, shiny, dull, furry or scaly. Here are some simple tips to help you give your drawings texture:

OLD AND RUSTY

To make a robot look old and rusty, add dirty streaks of oil and patches of rust. Use green and brown pens or paint.

SHINY AND NEW

To make a robot shine, add white highlights to one side of every edge. Then draw white patches with star shapes on them. Now your robot looks as if it's brand new!

HAIRY AND SCARY

To make a monster look furry, draw rough zigzags along the outline. Then, add more zigzag shapes to the body here and there.

SMOOTH AND SCALY

Add patches of small half circles at different points all over the monster's body. This will make the monster look scaly all over.

MEGAMORPH

Megamorph has huge metal wings and mighty arms and legs. This giant robot is easy to draw, but use a ruler as there are lots of straight lines.

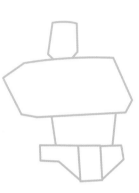

STEP 1

First, draw Megamorph's chest and lower body. Then add his small square head.

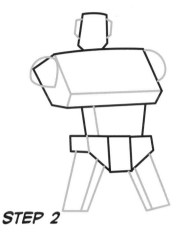

STEP 2

Now carefully draw Megamorph's shoulders and upper legs. Add ears and chest details.

STEP 3

Next, add his big shoulder guards and neck. Draw his rounded knees and chunky lower legs.

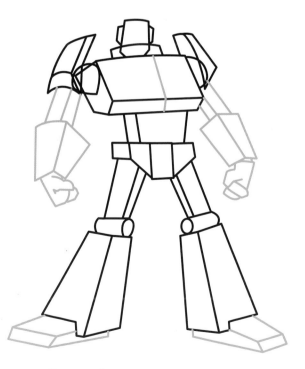

STEP 4

Add his arms, feet and mighty fists. Don't forget the line that goes down the middle of his chest.

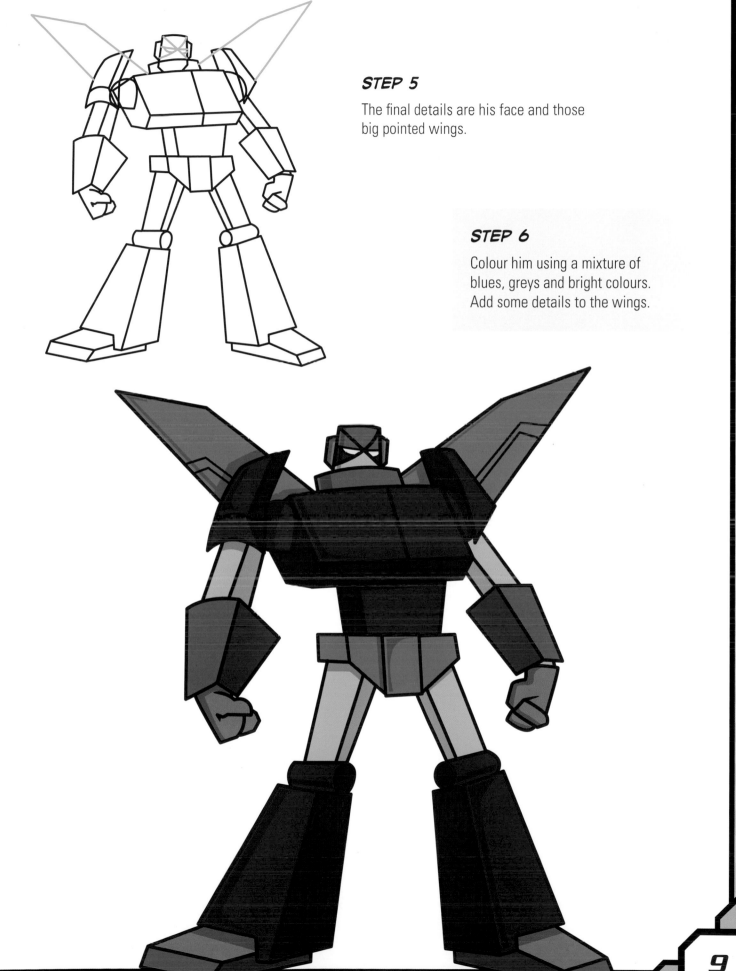

STEP 5

The final details are his face and those big pointed wings.

STEP 6

Colour him using a mixture of blues, greys and bright colours. Add some details to the wings.

DRAGON

Dragons are huge, fire-breathing monsters that look a lot like dinosaurs. They fly through the air flapping their enormous scaly wings.

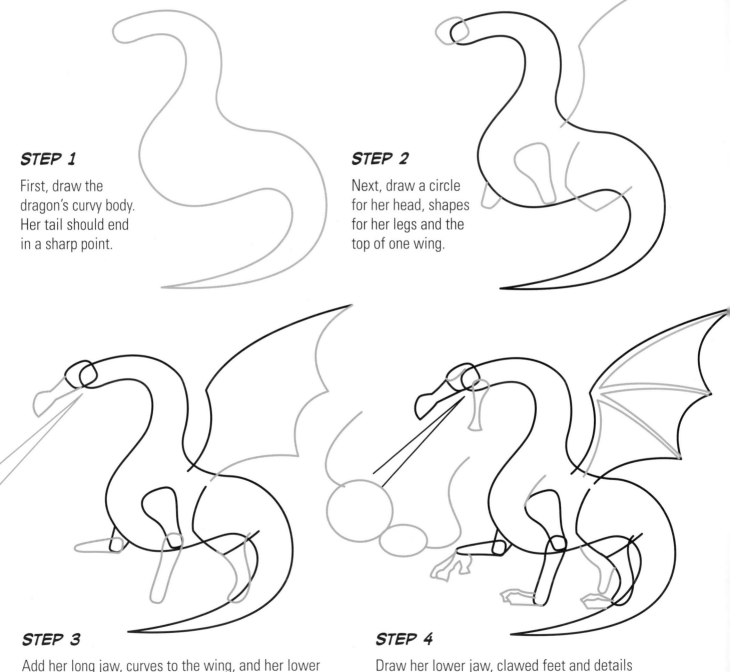

STEP 1

First, draw the dragon's curvy body. Her tail should end in a sharp point.

STEP 2

Next, draw a circle for her head, shapes for her legs and the top of one wing.

STEP 3

Add her long jaw, curves to the wing, and her lower legs. The two lines coming from her head are the beginning of her fiery breath.

STEP 4

Draw her lower jaw, clawed feet and details to her wing. Add two circles and wavy lines for her fiery breath.

STEP 5

Bring your dragon to life by adding her razor-sharp teeth, claws, her second wing and the details to her head. Don't forget the claw on her wing. Then, finish her dragon breath.

SUPER TIP!

A dragon's wing looks a lot like an umbrella. Draw four lines joining at a point. Turn them into spikes. Add a claw and curved lines at the bottom.

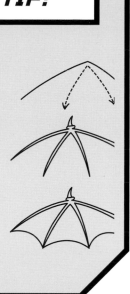

STEP 6

Add the triangular spines that run along the dragon's back. Then finish her off in bold, bright colours.

FUNNY ALIEN

This creature is called 'Blinky'. He is an alien monster with seven googly eyes. He has a big, friendly grin and thick, orange fur.

STEP 1

First, draw this shape to make your monster's body.

STEP 2

Add Blinky's wide head. Then draw his arms – one long and one curved.

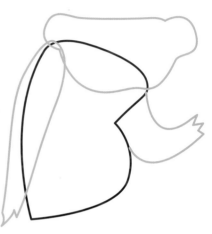

STEP 3

Now it's time to add lots of circles for his eyes. Then draw his legs, leaving a jagged line for his fur.

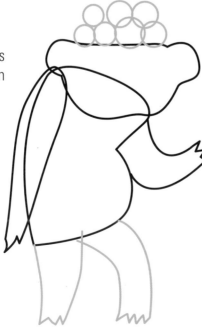

STEP 4

Add big, chunky hands and feet. Draw on claws. Give him a tuft of hair on top of his head.

STEP 5

Dot his body with shaggy tufts of fur. Then give him a wide, toothy grin. Draw black pupils on his eyes. Put them in different positions to make him look really monstrous.

STEP 6

Finish off your monster by colouring him in. The brighter, the better!

RETRO ROBOT

Retro Robot is a happy, shiny robot . He is always ready to lend a helping metal hand. Retro Robot has a wide toothy smile, bendy arms and large, clunky feet.

STEP 1

Start by copying these shapes for your robot's head and body.

STEP 2

Add small circles for his shoulders and hips, before drawing his long, skinny legs.

STEP 3

Draw his big eyes and wide mouth. Then add his long, bendy arms.

STEP 4

Give him an antenna, hands and feet. Don't forget that toothy grin.

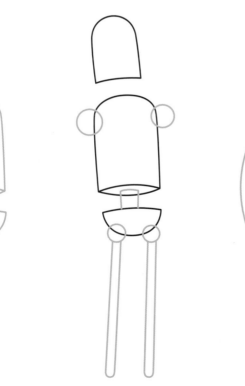

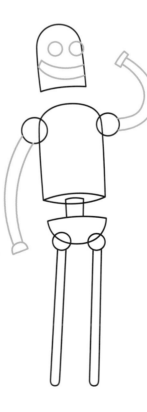

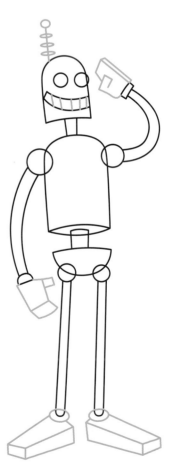

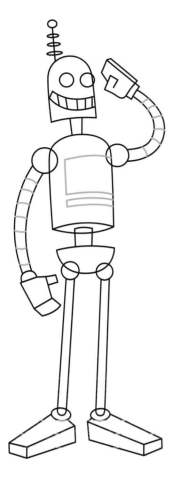

STEP 5

Now it's time to add the final details to his arms and body.

STEP 6

Finally, add big black dots to give him googly eyes, before colouring him in.

SUPER TIP!

- Not all robots have faces like people. Here is a different head that will make your robot look more like a machine.

- You can add little cameras and lights like this. He doesn't look so friendly now, does he?

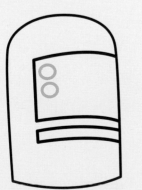

FRANKENSTEIN'S MONSTER

This monster is a crazy science experiment gone wrong! Dr Frankenstein made this creature by joining bits of bodies together with metal bolts. Now it's your turn to make him!

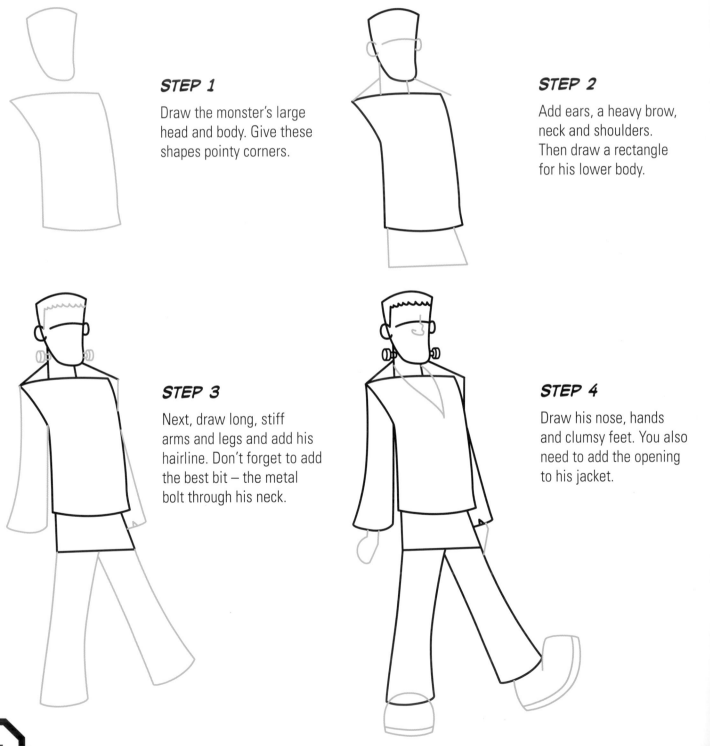

STEP 1

Draw the monster's large head and body. Give these shapes pointy corners.

STEP 2

Add ears, a heavy brow, neck and shoulders. Then draw a rectangle for his lower body.

STEP 3

Next, draw long, stiff arms and legs and add his hairline. Don't forget to add the best bit – the metal bolt through his neck.

STEP 4

Draw his nose, hands and clumsy feet. You also need to add the opening to his jacket.

STEP 5

Draw his fingers, before adding the details to his face and clothes. Don't forget the big scar across his forehead.

STEP 6

Your monster is now ready to colour. Use a gross green colour for his skin. GRRRRR!

AXEL R-8

Axel R-8 is a superfast robot that was built for speed. With his rocket-powered jet pack on his back, he's always ready for blast-off.

STEP 1

First, draw these shapes for your robot's head, chest and lower body.

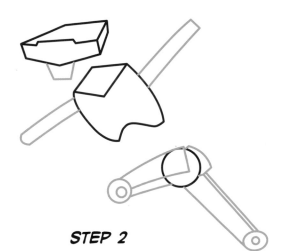

STEP 2

Draw long rectangles for his arms and add his face. Then draw the robotic legs.

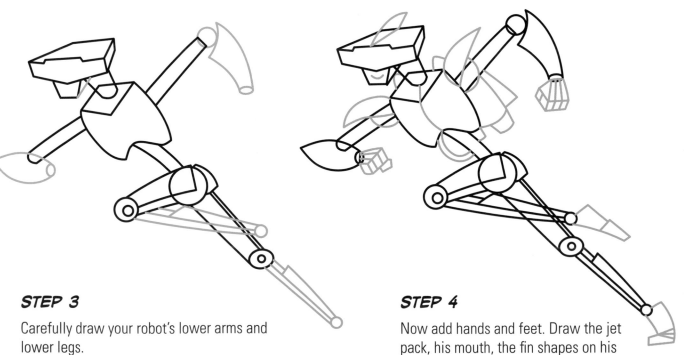

STEP 3

Carefully draw your robot's lower arms and lower legs.

STEP 4

Now add hands and feet. Draw the jet pack, his mouth, the fin shapes on his shoulders and head, and some of the other small details.

STEP 5

Add the final details to his head, neck and body.

STEP 6

Draw flames shooting out of the jet pack. Then colour in your racing robot!

COMPACTO THE CRUSHERBOT

Compacto moves around on big, rolling caterpillar tracks. He has huge, crushing plates instead of hands. His mission? To crush anything that gets in his way!

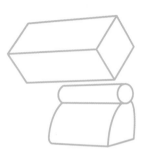

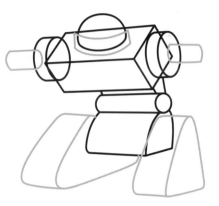

STEP 1

Begin by drawing a large block for his chest, a tube shape for his waist and curved shape for his lower body.

STEP 2

Next, draw his head and round shoulders. Then add lines to join the two parts of his body.

STEP 3

Draw a caterpillar track on either side of his body. Add upper arms and a neckband.

STEP 4

Add the circles that turn the track around. Then draw his heavy metal arms.

STEP 5

Now it's time to add the eyes and other details, including the heavy crushing plates.

STEP 6

Add the final details to the tracks and other parts of the Crusherbot. He's now ready to colour in.

SUPER TIP!

Follow these instructions to make your robot look like he's really pounding the ground:

- Start with your basic crushing plate shape. Add some small lines to show the impact on the ground.

- If you want to show even more destruction, add some long cracks between the lines.

- You can even add some small puffs of smoke to really finish it off.

Q-T BOT

Q-T Bot is the perfect robot friend. His special antennae mean you can call him any time you need help. This cheerful robot may be small, but he's stronger than he looks!

STEP 1

Use a coin to draw a big circle for his head. Then use a ruler to copy these shapes for his body and thighs.

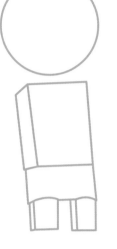

STEP 2

Take your time to draw his upper arms and lower legs. Don't forget to leave room for his big robot feet.

STEP 3

Now add lower arms, feet and big googly eyes. You also need to draw a line down the side of the leg on the right.

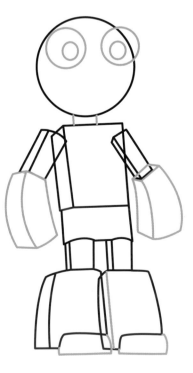

STEP 4

Give Q-T Bot a little mouth and helmet. Then draw shoulders, arm joints and a line for his waist.

STEP 5

Add chunky fingers, earphones and antennae. Draw a line down the side of his pants.

STEP 6

Finally, draw a planet on his chest and colour him in. We've used blue, but you could choose any colour.

WEREWOLF

In horror stories, a werewolf is a creature that's part human, part wolf. He has a man's body and wolf-like features such as a long bushy tail and razor-sharp teeth.

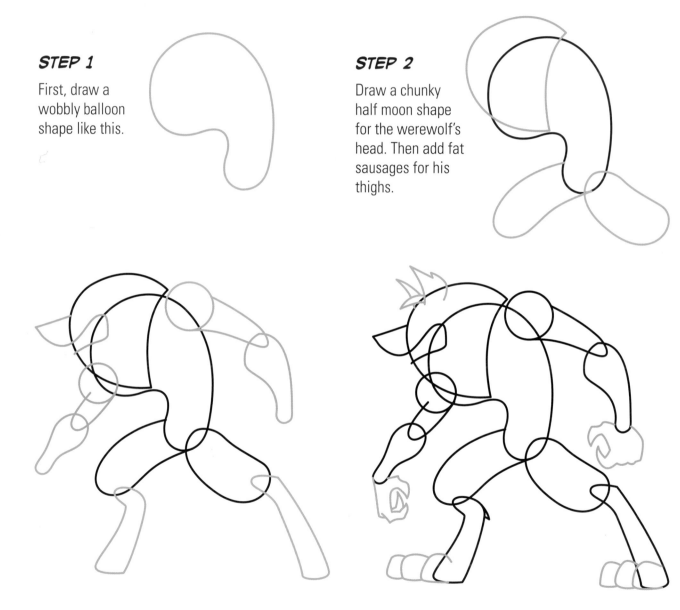

STEP 1

First, draw a wobbly balloon shape like this.

STEP 2

Draw a chunky half moon shape for the werewolf's head. Then add fat sausages for his thighs.

STEP 3

Draw his long muzzle and mouth, his shoulders and arms, and lower legs.

STEP 4

Next, draw his hairy ears, hands and big wolf feet.

STEP 5

Now it's time to add his long tail, eyes and ragged trousers. Then add lots of tufty bits of fur.

STEP 6

When you colour in your werewolf, remember to add lots of shading to make him really stand out. AWOOOOOOOO!

MEDIBOT

Medibot is a caring robot that can hover on the spot. She has a smiley face and carries a useful medical tray. Medibot is handy for when you're feeling poorly!

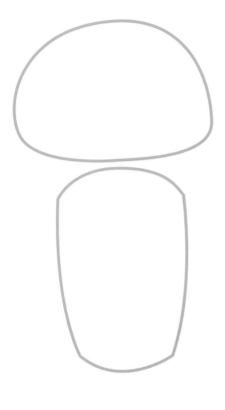

STEP 1

Firstly, draw a wide oval shape for her head. Now add a longer shape for her body.

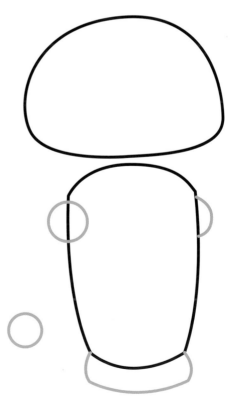

STEP 2

Add three little circles for her shoulders and elbows. Add a waistband.

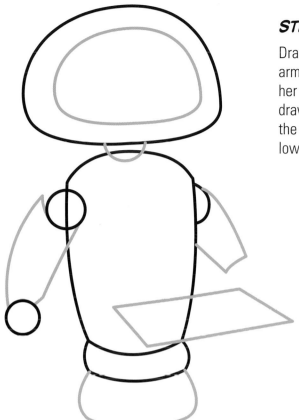

STEP 3

Draw your robot's upper arms and the outline of her face. Use a ruler to draw the tray. Then add the neck and her lower waistband.

STEP 4

Add three simple shapes for Medibot's smiley face. Then draw lower arms.

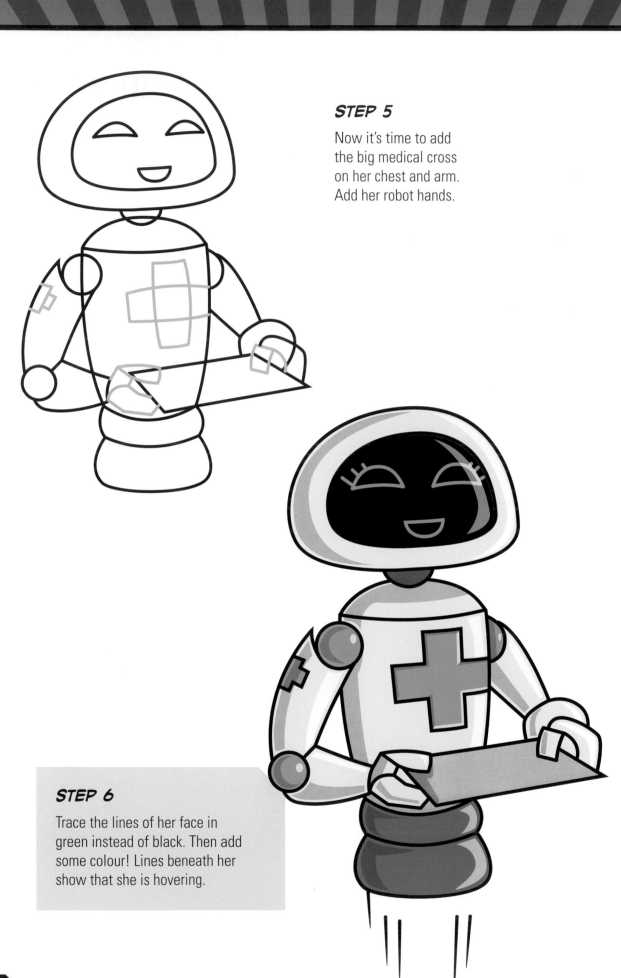

STEP 5

Now it's time to add the big medical cross on her chest and arm. Add her robot hands.

STEP 6

Trace the lines of her face in green instead of black. Then add some colour! Lines beneath her show that she is hovering.

With her well-cut suit and shiny black hair, Vampire Girl looks chic and stylish. But stay away from those fangs… because this girl bites!

STEP 1

Begin by drawing her slim body and head. Add a pointed ear.

STEP 2

Draw long legs followed by her thin arms.

STEP 3

Join her head and body with a neck. Continue the lines of her neck to make the front opening of her jacket, and add her hands.

STEP 4

Give her a wide collar, large cuffs and a belt buckle. Then add her long, straight hair.

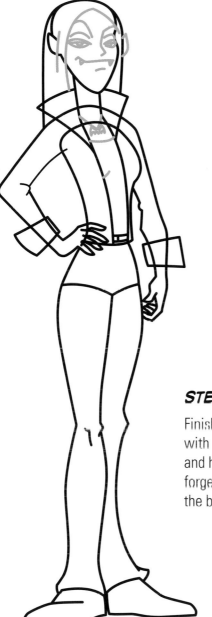

STEP 5

Finish off your drawing with her vampire face and hairline. Don't forget her fangs and the bat necklace.

STEP 6

Now colour Vampire Girl using dark, dangerous colours!

GLOSSARY

antenna An aerial that sends out or picks up signals.

brow Forehead.

cuff The end part of a sleeve, around the wrist.

fiery Burning and hot.

hairline The shape of the edge of the hair around the head.

HB A pencil with a lead that is neither hard nor soft, but somewhere in between.

muzzle The nose and mouth of an animal such as a horse or dog.

pupil The dark centre part of the eye.

rust The brown, flaky stuff that appears on metal when it is covered with water.

spine A spike.

vampire In stories, a dead person who leaves the grave to bite and suck the blood of living people.

FURTHER READING

How to Draw Monsters with Calvin Innes by Calvin Innes (My Little Big Town, 2014)

Ralph Masiello's Robot Drawing Book by Ralph Masiello (Charlesbridge Publishing, 2011)

What to Doodle? Robots and Superheroes by Peter Donahue (Dover Children's, 2013)

WEBSITES

www.dragoart.com/robots-c401-1.htm

www.hellokids.com/t_1295/robot

www.sciencekids.co.nz/robots.html

INDEX